The Formac Pocketguide to

WHALE
WATCHING

on Canada's East Coast

Written & illustrated by
Jeffrey C. Domm

Formac Publishing Company Limited
Halifax, Nova Scotia

Formac Publishing Company Limited acknowledges the support of the cultural affairs section, Nova Scotia Department of Tourism and Culture. We acknowledge the financial support of the Government of Canada through the Book Publishing Industry Development Program (BPIDP) for our publishing activities. We acknowledge the support of the Canada Council for the Arts for our publishing program.

National Library of Canada Cataloguing in Publication

Domm, Jeffrey C., 1958-
        Formac pocketguide to whale watching on Canada's east coast / written and illustrated by Jeffrey C. Domm.

Includes index.
ISBN 0-88780-597-3

        1. Whale watching—Atlantic Provinces—Guidebooks. 2. Whale watching—Atlantic Coast (Canada)—Guidebooks. 3. Whales—Atlantic Provinces—Identification. 4. Whales—Atlantic Coast (Canada)—Identification. I. Title.

QL737.C4D64 2003   599.5'09715   C2003-902160-2

Formac Publishing Company Limited
5502 Atlantic Street
Halifax, Nova Scotia
B3H 1G4
www.formac.ca

Printed and bound in Canada

Contents

How to Use This Book

This book is designed to simplify the process of identifying wildlife from a boat, whether you are on a whale watching excursion, sailing on a yacht or on a ferry crossing.

These are the visual keys in this book:

Dive Sequence shows what silhouette you will see above the water when the animal surfaces.

Habitat

 Inshore — close to the shore

 Offshore — several kilometres away from land

 Estuaries — in the mouth of a river

 Islands — around or on islands

Species

Atlantic Puffin
Atl. White-side
Basking Shark
Beluga
Black Guillem
Bluefin Tuna
Blue Shark
Blue Whale
Com. Bottleno
Common Eider
Common Tern
Cuvier's Beake
Dble.-crested
Fin Whale
Grt. Black-back
Great Cormora
Greater Shear
Great White Sh
Grey Seal
Harbour Porpois
Harbour Seal
Herring Gull
Humpback Wha
Leatherback
Loggerhead
Long-finned Pilo
Minke Whale
Moon Jellyfish
N. Bottlenose Wh

Contents

How to Use This Book

This book is designed to simplify the process of identifying wildlife from a boat, whether you are on a whale watching excursion, sailing on a yacht or on a ferry crossing.

These are the visual keys in this book:

Dive Sequence shows what silhouette you will see above the water when the animal surfaces.

Habitat

 Inshore — close to the shore

 Offshore — several kilometres away from land

 Estuaries — in the mouth of a river

 Islands — around or on islands

Threats

 Whaling/Hunting — caught by whalers

 Fishing — caught by fisherman

 Human Disturbance — where human activity, from walking to road building, disturbs the animal

 Fishing nets — fish, sea mammals and birds get caught in fishing nets

 Pollution — dumping of industrial and domestic waste are the most common kinds of pollution

 Loss of Habitat — the place where this animal breeds has been destroyed

Blow
Each species of whale has its own distinctive blow. This is the single most important identifying detail.

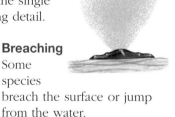

Breaching
Some species breach the surface or jump from the water.

Spyhopping
Vertically raising the head out of the water, usually while stationary, to view surrounding area.

Whale Watching in Atlantic Canada

The best way to see whales involves taking a boat trip out on the ocean. (You can occasionally see whales from shore, but it's not something you can rely on.) There are boat owners throughout Atlantic Canada who specialize in whale-watching tours.

If you want to see a specific kind of whale, you need to go where that whale lives and can find food, and you need to go at the right time of year. For example, if you set out on the Bay of Fundy, your chances of spotting a Right Whale are better than if you are on the Atlantic Ocean. To see a Bottlenose Whale, it's the other way around.

Use the locator map to determine which species you are most likely to see on the whale-watching trip in your region. Find the region on the map, then check the chart on pages 8 and 9 to see which species are common in the area.

Your best plan is to ask the cruise operators what kinds of whales they are seeing on their trips. The season of the year, the weather and the whales' supply of food all affect what creatures you are likely to see.

Brier Island Whale and Seabird Cruises

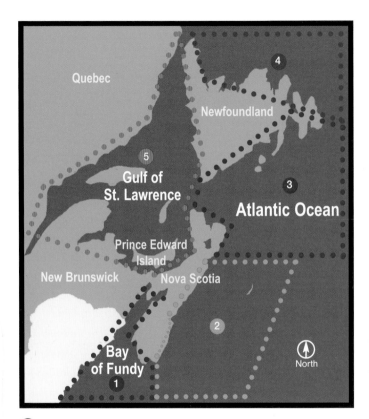

1. Bay of Fundy
2. Atlantic Coast/Nova Scotia (N.S.)
3. Cape Breton & South Coast/Newfoundland (NF)
4. North Coast/Newfoundland (NF)
5. Gulf of St. Lawrence

Species	Bay of Fundy	Atlantic Coast N.S.	C.B./S. Coast NF	North Coast NF	Gulf of St. Lawrence
Atlantic Puffin	●	⌒	●	●	⌒
Atl. White-sided Dolphin	●	◑	◑	◑	○
Basking Shark	●	◑	◑	◑	
Beluga					○
Black Guillemot	●	○	●	●	○
Bluefin Tuna	●	◑	◑	◑	◑
Blue Shark	◑	◑	◑	◑	◑
Blue Whale	⌒	◑	●	◑	○
Com. Bottlenose Dolphin	⌒	⌒			
Common Eider	●	○	●	●	○
Common Tern	●	○	●	●	○
Cuvier's Beaked Whale	⌒				
Dble.-crested Cormorant	●	○	●	●	○
Fin Whale	●	○	●	●	○
Grt. Black-backed Gull	●	○	●	●	○
Great Cormorant	◑	○	●	●	○
Greater Shearwater	●	○	●	●	○
Great White Shark	◑	◑			
Grey Seal	●	●	●	●	○
Harbour Porpoise	●	●	◑	◑	◑
Harbour Seal	●	○	●	●	○
Herring Gull	●	○	●	●	○
Humpback Whale	●	◑	●	●	⌒
Leatherback	⌒	⌒	⌒	⌒	
Loggerhead	⌒	⌒	⌒		
Long-finned Pilot Whale	⌒	⌒	●	●	
Minke Whale	●	○	●	●	○
Moon Jellyfish	◑	◑	◑	◑	◑
N. Bottlenose Whale		●			

See locator map, page 7

Species	Bay of Fundy	Atlantic Coast N.S.	C.B./ S. Coast NF	North Coast NF	Gulf of St. Lawrence
Northern Fulmar	●	●	●	●	●
Northern Gannet	●	●	●	●	●
Northern Right Whale	●	▲			
Ocean Sunfish	◒	▲	▲	▲	▲
Orca (Killer Whale)	▲	▲	▲	◒	
Porbeagle Shark	●	●	●	●	●
Portuguese Man-of-War		◒	◒	◒	●
Razorbill	●	◒	◒	◒	◒
Risso's Dolphin		◒	◒	◒	
Sailfish	▲	▲	▲	▲	▲
Sei Whale	▲	▲	●	▲	▲
Shortfin Mako	▲	●			
Sooty Shearwater	●	●	●	●	●
Sperm Whale	▲	▲	◒	▲	
Swordfish		▲	◒	▲	▲
Thresher Shark	▲	◒	◒	◒	◒
Tiger Shark	▲	◒			
Whale Shark	▲	▲	▲		▲
White-beaked Dolphin	▲	▲		●	
Wilson's Storm-Petrel	◒	◒	◒	◒	◒

● Most common in region
◒ Less common to region
▲ Rare to region
  Not found in region

See locator map, page 7

Rare Sightings

All species found in the additional species listings should be considered rare or transient only.

Northern Right Whale

BEHAVIOUR
- Slow swimmer, no dorsal fin
- Very acrobatic, breaches
- "V" shaped blow when surfacing
- Rolls on surface of water, waves flipper
- Approachable and inquisitive
- Raises fluke before diving

1 Large yellow/white callosities on head

2 Strongly arched mouth line curving down below eye

3 Largest callosities above eye

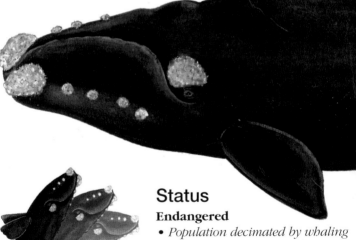

Breach Sequence

Status
Endangered
- *Population decimated by whaling*
- *Many deaths caused by ships and fishing gear entanglement*

HABITAT   THREATS

10

Dive Sequence

④ Round black body mottled brown, grey or blue

⑤ Finless dark back with no callosities

⑥ Flippers are broad and spatula-shaped

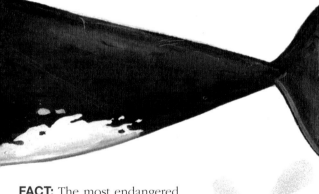

FACT: The most endangered whale found off coast, with only 300-350 animals known.

FAMILY: Balaenidae
Eubalaena glacialis

Blow

LENGTH 17 metres (57 ft)	WEIGHT 40,000 kg (90,000 lb)

Humpback Whale

BEHAVIOUR
- Raises fluke before diving
- Breaching reveals huge flippers
- Lifts head out of water to spyhop
- Rolls in water
- Curious, approaches boats

1. Small bumps on head and lower jaw

2. Flesh knobby with some barnacles

3. Extremely long, dark and light flippers

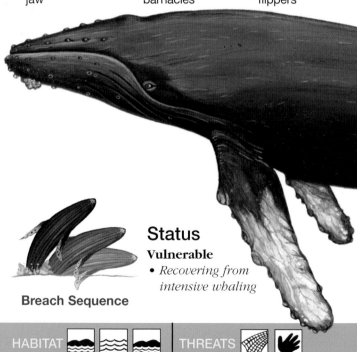

Breach Sequence

Status
Vulnerable
- *Recovering from intensive whaling*

HABITAT 〰 〰 〰 THREATS

12

Dive Sequence

④ Small, hump-like dorsal fin   ⑤ White pattern on underside of fluke   ⑥ Fluke serrated along back edge

FACT: Male creates sounds that can travel for up to 100 km (60 miles).

FAMILY: Balaenopteridae
Megaptera novaeangliae

Blow

| LENGTH 17 metres (57 ft) | WEIGHT 40,000 kg (90,000 lb) |

Minke Whale

BEHAVIOUR
- Does not raise fluke when diving
- Blow barely visible
- Unique dive sequence: blowhole and dorsal fin visible at same time
- Surfaces, blows and rolls in water
- Curious, approaches boats

1 Sharply pointed snout

2 Ridge along top of nose

3 Distinctive white band on flipper, sometimes pure black

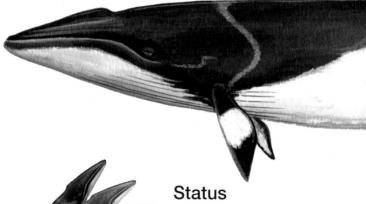

Breach Sequence

Status

Common
- *Currently hunted*
- *Actual numbers not known*

HABITAT   THREATS

Dive Sequence

④ Small sleek body, fin well forward

⑤ Colouring varies, from dark to light

⑥ Pointed fluke with notch

FACT: Minke populations range from 500,000 to 1,000,000, and are regularly hunted.

FAMILY: Balaenopteridae
Balaenoptera acutorostrata

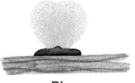

Blow

LENGTH	M 9.8 metres (32 ft) F 10.7 metres (35 ft)	WEIGHT	9200 kg (20,000 lb)

Sei Whale

BEHAVIOUR
- Does not raise fluke when diving
- Rarely arches back when diving
- Large dorsal fin located well back, prominent when surfacing
- Skims surface steadily when feeding
- Quick, small, compact blow

① Single ridge tops narrow nose to blowhole

② Uniform colouring on sides of head

③ Small white spots overall

Status
Vulnerable
- *Slight increase in numbers due to whaling restrictions*

Breach Sequence

HABITAT   THREATS

Dive Sequence

4 Erect, backward-curved dorsal fin, well back

5 Narrow flippers

6 Body dark grey overall

FACT: Often mistaken for shark because dorsal fin seen with very little back showing.

FAMILY: Balaenopteridae
Balaenoptera borealis

Blow

LENGTH	M 19.5 metres (64 ft) F 21 metres (69 ft)	WEIGHT	45,000 kg (100,000 lb)

Fin Whale

BEHAVIOUR
- Rarely raises fluke when diving
- Swims on side with mouth open to feed on surface prey
- Rarely breaches or spyhops
- Travels alone or in pairs

1 White on lower right side of head, black on lower left

2 "V" shaped pattern behind head

3 Extremely long, dark grey body overall

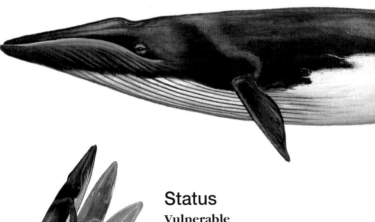

Status
Vulnerable
- *Intensively whaled in past*

Breach Sequence

HABITAT   THREATS

Dive Sequence

④ Dorsal fin small and well back

⑤ Various markings on dorsal fin

⑥ Broad fluke with pointed lobes

FACT: Second largest living animal after the blue whale, record length 27 metres (88 feet).

FAMILY: Balaenopteridae
Balaenoptera physalus

Blow

LENGTH 24 metres (79 ft)	WEIGHT 120,000 kg (265,000 lb)

Blue Whale

BEHAVIOUR
- Blows up to fifteen times before diving
- Tall, thick two-column blow
- Raises fluke when diving
- Slow swimmer
- Usually swims just below surface
- Pairs swim spaced well apart

1 Pointed nose   **2** Flat, "U" shaped head   **3** Small bumps in front of blowhole

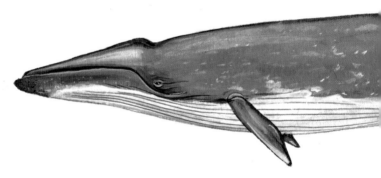

Status

Endangered
- *Recovering from intensive whaling*

HABITAT THREATS

Dive Sequence

④ Small hook on dorsal fin

⑤ Small dorsal fin set very far back on body

⑥ Large whale, mottled grey/ blue body

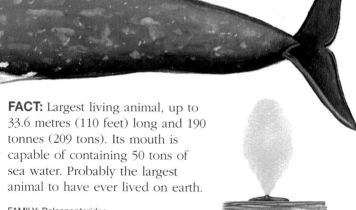

FACT: Largest living animal, up to 33.6 metres (110 feet) long and 190 tonnes (209 tons). Its mouth is capable of containing 50 tons of sea water. Probably the largest animal to have ever lived on earth.

FAMILY: Balaenopteridae
Balaenoptera musculus

Blow

| LENGTH 29.8 metres (98 ft) | WEIGHT 180,000 kg (400,000 lb) |

Sperm Whale

BEHAVIOUR
- Loud first exhalation after surfacing
- Very strong blow projected forward and to left
- Raises fluke before diving
- Often dives and surfaces in same place
- Dives for long periods, typically 45 minutes.
- After long dive, remains motionless on surface

1 Square head with barely visible lower jaw

2 Blowhole slightly raised on left side of head

3 Body often badly scarred near head

Breach Sequence

Status
Vulnerable
- *Currently threatened by human activity*

HABITAT THREATS

Dive Sequence

④ Body dark grey overall with white patches around mouth and belly

⑤ Low, hump-like dorsal fin

⑥ Small knuckles between fin and tail

FACT: World's largest toothed whale. Routinely dives to 750 m (2,400 feet) in pursuit of giant deep-water squid. Recorded dives to 2800 m (9,000 feet).

FAMILY: Physeteridae
Physeter macrocephalus

Blow

| LENGTH 18 metres (60 ft) | WEIGHT 45,000 kg (100,000 lb) |

Cuvier's Beaked Whale

BEHAVIOUR
- Back heavily arched when sounding
- Swims in groups of 10 or fewer
- Dives for 10-15 minutes

1 Two teeth extend from lower jaw, males only

2 Gently sloping white forehead

3 Robust body can be grey, black, brown or blue

Breach

Status
Unknown
- *Found in all oceans except polar waters*

HABITAT

THREATS

24

Swimming

④ Dorsal fin curved backward, well down back. Small flippers

⑤ White/grey across back

⑥ White scars usually cover body

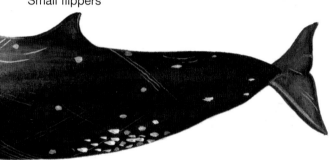

FACT: One of the most widespread and abundant beaked whales in the world.

FAMILY: Ziphiidae
Ziphius caviorstris

Blow

| LENGTH 6.9 metres (23 ft) | WEIGHT 2000 kg (4000 lb) |

Northern Bottlenose Whale

BEHAVIOUR
- Rests with beak and part of forehead extended out of water
- Very curious, approaches boats
- Swims in small groups

1 Large round forehead with white patch

2 Long, prominent tube-like beak

3 Female has white collar on neck

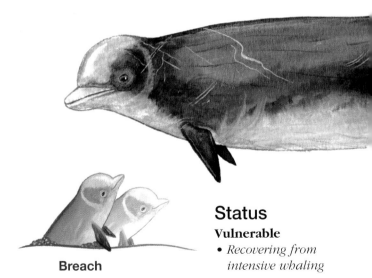

Breach

Status

Vulnerable
- *Recovering from intensive whaling*

HABITAT   THREATS

Swimming

④ Small, hooked dorsal fin set well back

⑤ Body sometimes mottled brown-grey or yellowish-brown

⑥ Fluke has pointed lobes

FACT: Found regularly on the continental shelf. Population of about 230 whales year-round. Spends entire year in cold waters.

FAMILY: Ziphiidae
Hyperoodon ampullatus

Spyhop

| LENGTH 9.8 metres (32 ft) | WEIGHT | Estimates only (several tons) |

Beluga

BEHAVIOUR
- Very agile, flexible neck
- Very expressive facial expressions
- Surfaces often, moves slowly and gently
- Spyhops, shows curiosity to boats
- Travels in groups of 5-20 animals

❶ Small, rounded forehead   **❷** Short beak   **❸** Flexible neck moves side to side

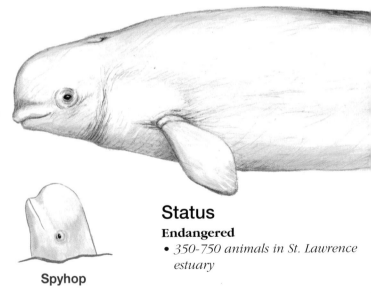

Spyhop

Status
Endangered
- *350-750 animals in St. Lawrence estuary*

HABITAT  THREATS

28

Dive Sequence

④ Small dorsal ridge, no fin

⑤ Small, broad flippers

⑥ Only white whale in Gulf of St. Lawrence

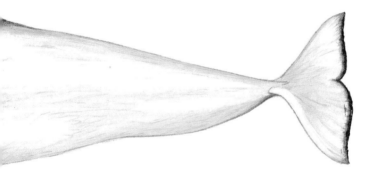

FACT: Sailors named Belugas "sea canaries" because of the array of sounds — croaks, whistles and brays — produced by an air sac in head.

FAMILY: Monodontidae
Delphinapterus leucas

| LENGTH 5.5 metres (18 ft) | WEIGHT 1600 kg (3500 lb) |

Common Bottlenose Dolphin

BEHAVIOUR
- Very acrobatic: bodysurfs, rides bow waves, splashes tail
- Leaps from water at high speeds
- Often rides pressure waves made by moving boats
- Seen mostly near shore and in estuaries
- Very curious, approaches boats
- Lives in large groups of 100 or more

1 Round forehead with medium-length beak

2 Slight ridge running up forehead

3 Robust body grey overall, muted colouring

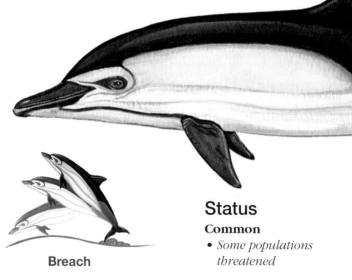

Breach

Status

Common
- *Some populations threatened*

HABITAT   THREATS

Swimming

④ Prominent large, curved dorsal fin ⑤ Pointed flippers ⑥ Long tail with pointed fins

FACT: When hunting, dolphins will stun prey with their tails.

FAMILY: Delphinidae
Tursiops truncatus

Spyhop

LENGTH 3.5 metres (12 ft)	WEIGHT 500 kg (1100 lb)

White-beaked Dolphin

BEHAVIOUR
- Leaps from water and is extremely acrobatic
- Races around boats at high speed making distinctive "rooster tail" spray
- Very curious, approaches boats

1 Short thick white, black or grey beak

2 Black forehead

3 Very robust with exceptionally thick blubber layer

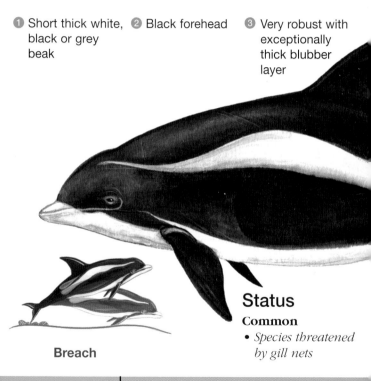

Breach

Status

Common
- *Species threatened by gill nets*

HABITAT THREATS

Swimming

④ Large, curved black dorsal fin

⑤ Dark flippers

⑥ Dark pointed lobes on fluke

FACT: Ventures into Arctic waters, further north than any other dolphin.

FAMILY: Delphinidae
Lagenorhynchus albirostris

Spyhop

| LENGTH 3 metre (10 ft) | WEIGHT 350 kg (770 lb) |

Atlantic White-sided Dolphin

BEHAVIOUR
- Dolphin most often seen jumping in boats' pressure waves
- Jumps clear out of water
- Travels in groups up to 100 animals
- Often accompanies feeding whales
- Breaches frequently

1 Short beak, black on top, white underside

2 White patch along side below dorsal fin

3 Black/dark grey on top

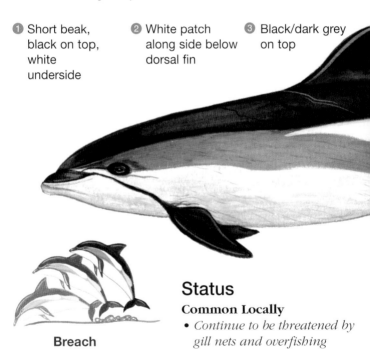

Breach

Status

Common Locally
- *Continue to be threatened by gill nets and overfishing*

HABITAT   THREATS

Swimming

④ Bright yellow patch along flanks at rear

⑤ Black line from beak to black pointed flippers

⑥ Pointed lobes on grey/black tail

FACT: Often accompanies other whales and dolphins in search of prey. Easily confused with white-beaked dolphin.

FAMILY: Delphinidae
Lagenorhynchus acutus

Spyhop

| LENGTH 2.8 metres (9 ft) | WEIGHT 230 kg (510 lb) |

Risso's Dolphin

BEHAVIOUR
- Swims with fin out of water, much like orca
- Younger animals occasionally breach, adults half-breach
- Occasionally spyhops
- Surfs in waves
- Typically dives for one to two minutes

1 No beak

2 Broad blunt head lighter grey

3 Robust body, grey overall, lightens with age

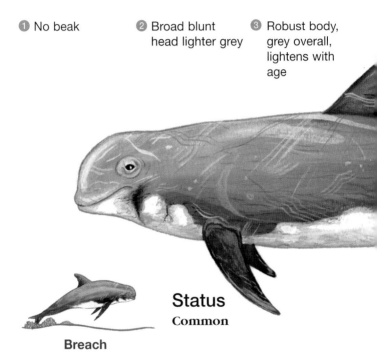

Status
Common

Breach

HABITAT THREATS

36

Swimming

④ Very tall, erect dorsal fin

⑤ Extreme scarring over entire body

⑥ All appendages — tail, flippers, dorsal fin — are dark

FACT: Largest species of dolphin. Sometimes mistaken for other larger species, such as orcas, because of large, curved dorsal fin.

FAMILY: Delphinidae
Grampus griseus

Spyhop

| LENGTH 4 metres (13 ft) | WEIGHT 500 kg (1,100 lb) |

Orca (Killer Whale)

BEHAVIOUR
- Activities include spyhopping, spouting loudly, breaching and lob-tailing
- Cruises in shallow water for prey
- Very talkative: clicks, whistles and bursts
- Curious, approaches boats

① Small beak, black on top, white bottom

② White patch along side of head

③ Large, black, round flippers

Breach

Status
Unknown
- *Hunted in recent years off Japan*

HABITAT	THREATS

Swimming

④ Tall erect dorsal fin, reaching 2 metres (7 feet)

⑤ Grey patch behind dorsal fin

⑥ Body black overall

FACT: Orcas live in pods of up to 40 whales.

FAMILY: Delphinidae
Orcinus orca

Spyhop

| LENGTH 9 metres (30 ft) | WEIGHT 5600 kg (12,000 lb) |

Long-finned Pilot Whale

BEHAVIOUR
- Often lies motionless, resting, at surface
- Occasionally rides bow waves
- Lob-tails and spyhops
- Swims in groups of 4-15 animals

1 Large forehead   **2** White line from eye to dorsal fin   **3** Dorsal fin positioned well forward

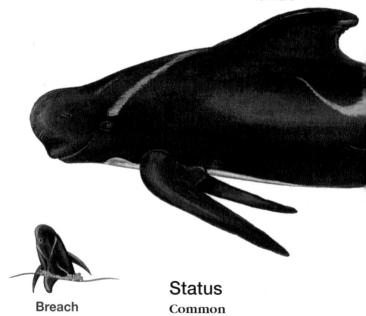

Breach

Status

Common

HABITAT

THREATS

Swimming

④ Broad dorsal fin with hooked tip.

⑤ White saddle behind dorsal fin

⑥ Long, dark flippers

FACT: Strandings of whole groups are common with this species. No one knows why, but one theory is that if leader becomes disoriented and beaches, remaining group members will follow.

FAMILY: Delphinidae
Globicephala melas

Spyhop

| LENGTH 6.3 metres (21 ft) | WEIGHT 2300 kg (5000 lb) |

41

Harbour Porpoise

BEHAVIOUR
- "Pop" sound when blowing
- Quick, splashless roll at surface
- Swims just below surface in shallow coastal waters
- Wary of boats and other activity
- Swims in small groups or alone

① Minimal beak

② Dark line from flipper to corner of mouth

③ Small body, dark grey overall

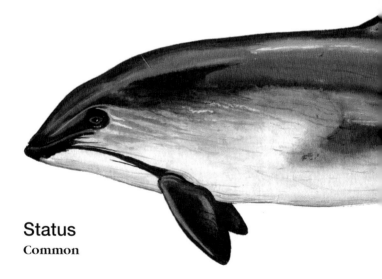

Status
Common

HABITAT   THREATS

Swimming

④ Small bumps extending up dorsal fin

⑤ Low triangular dorsal fin in middle of back

⑥ White sides and belly, greying towards top

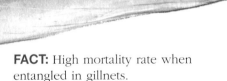

FACT: High mortality rate when entangled in gillnets.

FAMILY: Phocoenidae
Phocoena phocoena

Spyhop

LENGTH 1.6 metres (5.2 ft)	WEIGHT 63 kg (140 lb)

Harbour Seal

BEHAVIOUR
- Extends head out of water while breathing
- Climbs onto rocks and rocky beaches
- Frequents coastal lagoons and bays
- Pulls head straight down, no back showing on surface

1 Long broad nose with whiskers   **2** Tan to silver morphs   **3** Scattered darker spots

Status

Common

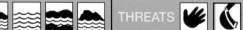

HABITAT   THREATS

④ Short, broad fore flippers

⑤ Round, short robust body with lighter underbelly

⑥ Males slightly larger than females

FACT: Seal pups can swim and dive within minutes of birth.

FAMILY: Phocidae
Phoca vitulina

Spyhop

| LENGTH 1.9 metres (6 ft) | WEIGHT 170 kg (370 lb) |

Grey Seal

BEHAVIOUR
- Gathers on islands and other shores to breed, molt and rest
- Often seen only as heads bobbing in water
- Backs occasionally break surface when diving to sea floor.

1 Long, broad, horse like snout with whiskers

2 Large, rotund chest

3 Colour difference between darker male and lighter female

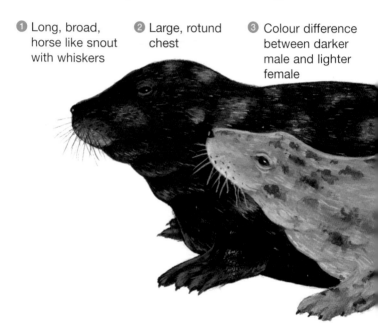

Status

Unknown
- *Have been hunted for many years, but numbers are steadily increasing*

HABITAT THREATS

❹ Body dark blue-grey overall with large dorsal fin

❺ Ridges across back to tail

❻ Two large lobes on tail fin

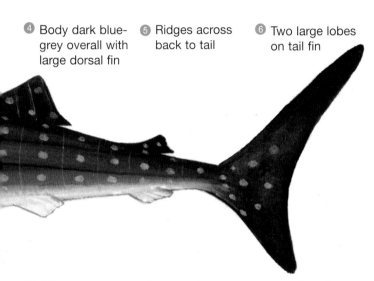

FACT: World's largest fish, reaching 20 metres in length (65 feet).

FAMILY: Rhincodontidae
Rhincodon typus

LENGTH 12 metres (39 ft) | WEIGHT 12,000 kg (26,500 lb)

Thresher Shark

BEHAVIOUR
- Swims at surface in coastal waters
- Slaps water with long tail fin
- Very fast swimmer

1 Large eyes   **2** Blunt snout   **3** Body dark blue/grey to black overall

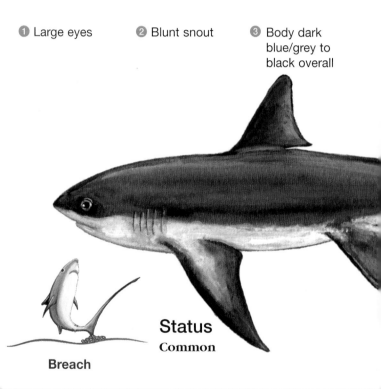

Status
Common

Breach

HABITAT   THREATS

Swimming

④ Very large, paddle-like pelvic fins

⑤ Second pectoral fin, slightly smaller than first

⑥ Extremely long upper tail section

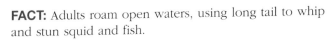

FACT: Adults roam open waters, using long tail to whip and stun squid and fish.

FAMILY: Alopiidae
Alopias vulpinus

| LENGTH 5.5 metres (18 ft) | WEIGHT 450 kg (990 lb) |

Basking Shark

BEHAVIOUR
- Swims slowly near surface when feeding
- Mouth gapes open when feeding on plankton, krill and small fish
- Tip of dorsal fin often flops over to one side
- Often seen near continental shelf
- Basks at surface in large groups

1 Small eyes for body size

2 Large, pointed snout

3 Often scarred around nose

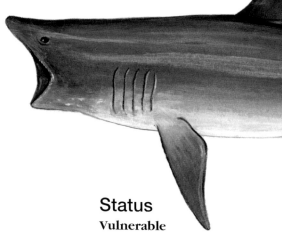

Status
Vulnerable
- *Once harvested for its flesh, oily liver and fins*

HABITAT THREATS

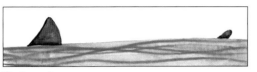

Swimming

④ Body dark blue/grey or brown overall

⑤ Large pectoral fin

⑥ White tip on top lobe of tail fin

FACT: Watch for two fins sitting still in the water. Although there are only a few reports, the Basking Shark will breach. Lives near bottom during colder months.

FAMILY: Cetorhinidae
Cetorhinus maximus

LENGTH **10 metres (33 ft)** WEIGHT **6000 kg (13,000 lb)**

Great White Shark

BEHAVIOUR
- Usually swims alone
- Slow swimmer with high speed sprints
- Jaws protrude when biting
- Third membrane rolls over eye for protection

1 Snout bluntly pointed   **2** Nose area scarred   **3** Large gill slits

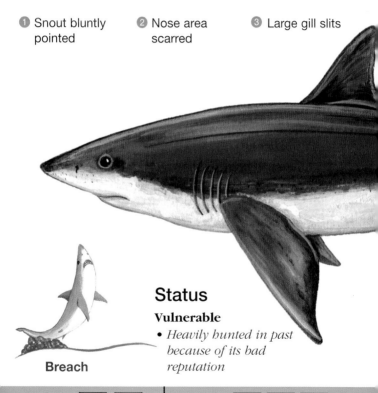

Status

Vulnerable
- *Heavily hunted in past because of its bad reputation*

Breach

HABITAT THREATS

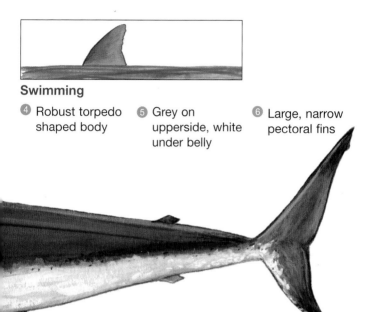

Swimming

④ Robust torpedo shaped body

⑤ Grey on upperside, white under belly

⑥ Large, narrow pectoral fins

FACT: Can regulate body temperature internally, allowing easy movement from cold to warmer waters.

FAMILY: Lamnidae
Carcharadon carcharias

LENGTH 7.3 metres (24 ft)	WEIGHT 2000 kg (4400 lb) or more

Shortfin Mako

BEHAVIOUR
- Can leap 6 metres (20 feet) out of water
- Very fast swimmer

❶ Long, pointed snout

❷ Teeth visible even when mouth is closed

❸ Spindle-shaped body

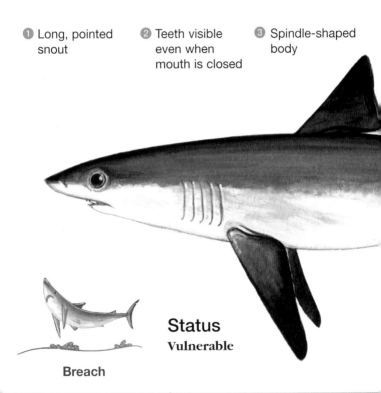

Breach

Status
Vulnerable

HABITAT   THREATS

Swimming

④ Body metallic blue

⑤ Large, erect dorsal fin

⑥ Large pectoral fins

FACT: Follows warm water currents of Gulf Stream preying on fish, especially mackerel and herring.

FAMILY: Lamnidae
Isurus oxyrinchus

| LENGTH 4 metres (13 ft) | WEIGHT 230 kg (500 lb) |

Porbeagle Shark

BEHAVIOUR
- Prefers deep water, depths up to
  350 metres (1200 feet).

① Short, pointed
nose

② Robust body

③ Very large dorsal
fin

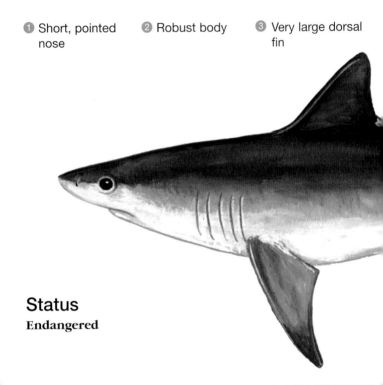

Status
Endangered

HABITAT THREATS

Swimming

④ Blueish-grey overall with paler underbelly

⑤ White hind tip of first dorsal fin

⑥ Large, crescent-shaped tail fin

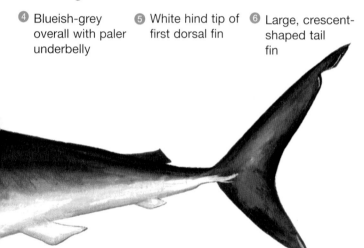

FACT: Among sharks, the most endangered by overfishing.

FAMILY: Lamnidae
Lamna nasus

| LENGTH 3.7 metres (12 ft) | WEIGHT 120 kg (265 lb) |

Tiger Shark

BEHAVIOUR
- Quick, sudden movements
- Slow, deliberate swimming

1 Tiger stripes running length of body and tail

2 Short, rounded nose

3 Body bluish-grey overall

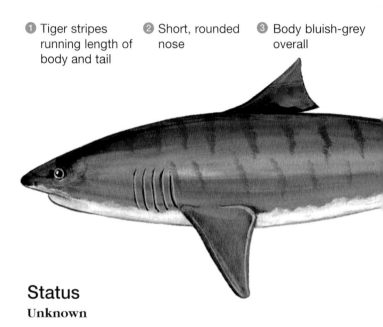

Status
Unknown

HABITAT   THREATS

Swimming

④ White underbelly ⑤ Large, broad pectoral fins, rounded at tips ⑥ Long, pointed tail fin; smaller lobe on bottom

FACT: Eats anything — bottles, car license plates, deer antlers — perhaps due to poor eyesight. Known as "goat of the ocean."

FAMILY: Carcharhinidae
Galeocerdo cuvier

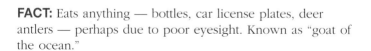

LENGTH 7.5 metres (25 ft) WEIGHT 900 kg (1990 lb)

Blue Shark

BEHAVIOUR
- Solitary swimmer
- Very quick, sudden movements

❶ Long snout, rounded at tip

❷ Large, round eyes with white rim

❸ Deep indigo overall with bluer sides

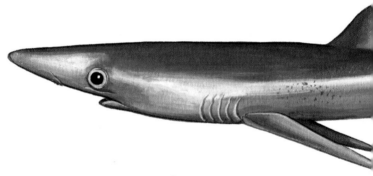

Status

Lower risk
- *Overfishing is beginning to have impact on species.*

HABITAT   THREATS

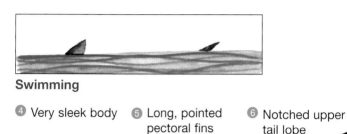

Swimming

④ Very sleek body   ⑤ Long, pointed pectoral fins   ⑥ Notched upper tail lobe

FACT: Most widely distributed shark found in three oceans. Known by several names: Blue Whaler, Great Blue Shark, Blue Dog.

FAMILY: Carcharhinidae
Prionace glauca

| LENGTH 3.8 metres (12.5 ft) | WEIGHT 200 kg (440 lb) |

Bluefin Tuna

BEHAVIOUR
- Fin breaks surface of water every 1-2 seconds
- Very fast swimmer, up to 80 km/h (50 mph)
- Often leaps from water after prey

① Sleek, strong body

② Hints of yellow on fins

③ Small ridge on top and bottom of tail area

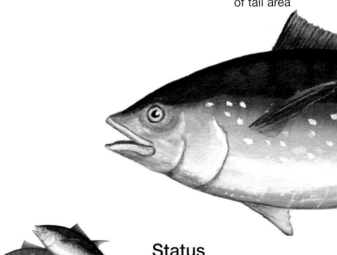

Breach

Status

Vulnerable
- *Overfishing threatens future stocks*

 HABITAT THREATS

Swimming

④ Dark upperside, blue to grey

⑤ Long second dorsal and pectoral fins

⑥ Long, sleek tail fin

FACT: Among largest of game fishes. Largest specimen weighed 680 kilograms (1500 pounds).

FAMILY: Scombridae
Thunnus thynnus

| LENGTH 4.3 metres (14 ft) | WEIGHT 910 kg (2,010 lb) |

Sailfish

BEHAVIOUR
- Very fast swimmer, dorsal fin occasionally breaks surface
- Occasionally feeds on surface prey

① Long, sword-like beak

② Long, streamlined body, tapered at rear

③ Large, spotted sail-like dorsal fin

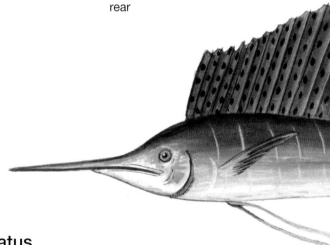

Status

Vulnerable
- *Overfishing could threaten stocks*

HABITAT | THREATS

Swimming

④ Long, thin pelvic fin

⑤ Dark blue body blends to brown-blue

⑥ Curved lateral line extending back to base of tail

FACT: Large sail-like dorsal fin is used in territorial fighting, mating, and herding schooling fish.

FAMILY: Istiophoridae
Istiophorus platypterus

LENGTH 2.9 metres (9.5 ft)	WEIGHT 70 kg (155 lb)

Swordfish

BEHAVIOUR
- Both dorsal and tail fins extend above surface
- Very fast swimmer, occasionally leaps from water
- Sometimes seen basking at surface

1 Long, flat sword-like upper jaw

2 Very high, rigid dorsal fin

3 Single keel on each side of body

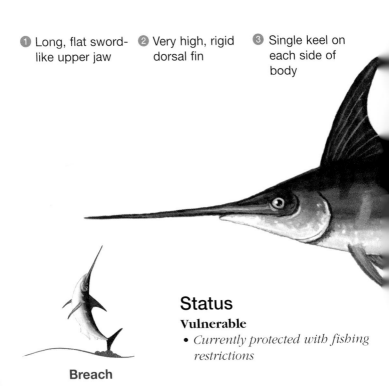

Breach

Status
Vulnerable
- *Currently protected with fishing restrictions*

HABITAT   THREATS

Swimming

④ Variable colours: black, greyish-blue, brown, bronze

⑤ Sides dusky-coloured

⑥ Lacks scales

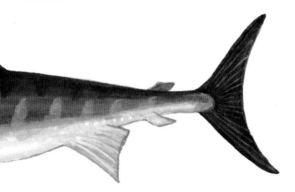

FACT: Hunts by plowing through schools of fish using sword-like upper jaw to stun and occasionally spear prey, in depths up to 920 metres (500 fathoms).

FAMILY: Xiphiidae
Xiphias gladius

| LENGTH 4.5 metres (15 ft) | WEIGHT 590 kg (1,300 lb) |

Ocean Sunfish

BEHAVIOUR
- Swims at surface, usually near flotsam or drifting kelp
- Fins stick out of water, often mistaken for sharks' fins
- Two large fins flap side to side for mobility
- Will lay flat and nearly motionless on ocean's surface
- Will approach swimmers

① Small mouth

② Extremely large body, no scales, appears as giant head

③ Colour ranges from dark grey to white, some mottling

④ Very long dorsal and anal fins

⑤ Body very flat and compressed, grey overall

⑥ Broad, short scalloped tail fin acts as rudder

Swimming

HABITAT THREATS

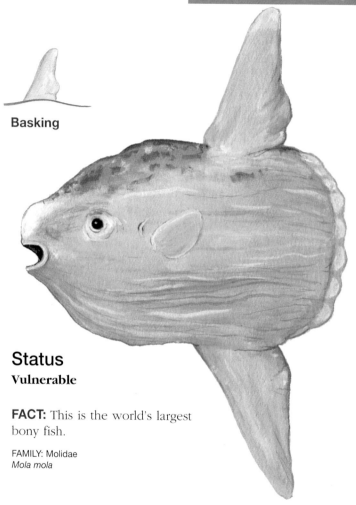

Basking

Status
Vulnerable

FACT: This is the world's largest bony fish.

FAMILY: Molidae
Mola mola

LENGTH 4 metres (13 ft)	WEIGHT 2000 kg (4400 lb)

Leatherback

BEHAVIOUR
- Large, quick breaths at surface
- Spends more time surfaced during night hours
- Dives extremely deep, up to 1000 metres (500 fathoms)
- Shallower dives at dusk, deeper at dawn

1 Black with tiny white spots overall

2 Extremely large, dark body

3 Long flippers

Dermochelys coriacea

Status

Endangered
- *Protected species. Threatened by illegal egg harvest.*

FACT: World's largest reptile. Turtles mistake floating plastic bags for jellyfish, causing harm when bags are swallowed.

LENGTH 1.6 metres (5 ft)	WEIGHT 360 kg (800 lb)
HABITAT	THREATS

Loggerhead

BEHAVIOUR
- Slow swimmer, floats near surface
- Lifts head out of water for breath
- Flaps large flippers in front just prior to diving

① Dark reddish brown pattern on head

② Dark brown heart-shaped shell

③ Front flippers longer than back

Status
Protected
- *Protected species.*

Caretta caretta

FACT: Rarer in North Atlantic waters but occasionally seen off southern tip of Nova Scotia.

LENGTH 122 cm (48 inches)	WEIGHT 70 kg (155 lb)
HABITAT	THREATS

Portuguese Man-of-War

BEHAVIOUR
- Floats on surface
- Float changes shape to catch wind direction
- Occasionally has fish swimming amongst tentacles

1 Large pink-ridged, sail-like crest

2 Dense cluster of tentacles underneath

3 Iridescent, pale blue and pink

4 Blue-black tentacles up to 19 metres (60 feet) long

Status

Common

FACT: Most poisonous of the jellyfish

Physalia physalis

FLOAT 30 cm (12 inches)

HABITAT

HEIGHT 15 cm (6 inches)
WIDTH 13 cm (5 inches)

THREATS

Moon Jellyfish

BEHAVIOUR
- Floats near surface
- Found on shore of sandy beaches washed up by tide
- Moves by pulsating action of the body

1 Saucer-shaped, translucent

2 Short, finger-like tentacles at end of bell

3 Horseshoe-shaped gonads on top

4 Colours: yellowish-pink, violet, rose and brown

Status

Common

FACT: The tentacles contain stinging cells, used for getting food and for self-defence.

Aurelia aurita

LENGTH	41 cm (16 inches)	HEIGHT	7 cm (3 inches)
HABITAT		THREATS	

Smooth Hammerhead

- Easily distinguished by square head. Only hammerhead in Canadian waters

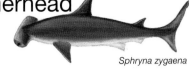

Sphryna zygaena

LENGTH **4 metres (13 ft)**

Spiny Dogfish

- Small schooling shark, may form groups of hundreds

Squalus acanthias

LENGTH **1 metre (3.3 ft)**

Oceanic Whitetip Shark

- Tip of dorsal fin mottled white, but some animals without distinctive markings

Carcharhinus longimanus

LENGTH **4 metres (13 ft)**

Sharksucker

- Attach themselves to whales, sharks and turtles, occasionally darting away to catch small fish

Echeneis naucrates

LENGTH **90 centimetres (3 ft)**

Dolphinfish (Mahi-Mahi)

- High forehead, dorsal fin running length of body, forked tail. Fast swimmer

Coryphaena hippurus

LENGTH **2 metres (6 ft)**

Atlantic Mackerel

- Small fish forming large schools, usually pursued by whales, dolphins or birds

Scomber scombrus

LENGTH 60 centimetres (2 ft)

Atlantic Flyingfish

- Small delicate fish with large wing-like fins that allows it to glide over surface of water.

Cypselurus melanurus

LENGTH 25 cm (1 1/2 feet)

Sea Gooseberry

- Found floating in large swarms in estuaries, bays, along rocky and sandy shores

Pleurobrachia bachei

WIDTH 25 millimetres (1 inch)

Angled Hydromedusa

- 60 long tentacles with yellowish-tan to reddish-brown base
- Found floating in bays, estuaries and along rocky shores

Gonionemus vertens

WIDTH 19 millimetres (3/4 inch)

Comb Jelly

- Floats in shallow waters near rocky shores

Mnemiopsis lediyi

WIDTH 51 millimetres (2 inches)

Greater Shearwater

BEHAVIOUR
- Erratic flight, towering and banking, with stiff choppy wingbeats
- Scavenges behind fishing vessels
- Rests in large flocks on water
- Swims underwater feeding on small fish and squid

❶ Black cap on head with white chin and cheeks

❷ Black beak

❸ Narrow wings in flight

❹ Dull grey-brown overall with white belly

Puffinus gravis

Status

Common
- *Numbers have been falling*

FACT: Lives far from shore. Commonly killed by storms with high winds and waves.

LENGTH 51 centimetres (20 inches)

HABITAT

THREATS

Sooty Shearwater

BEHAVIOUR
- Extremely graceful flyer, skimming low over water
- Long, narrow wings, similar to swift in flight
- Very stiff, quick wingbeats
- Usually flies alone or in very small groups

1 Slender black beak

2 Sleek body, sooty brown

3 Darkest on upper wings and tail feathers

4 Underside of wings grey in flight

Puffinus griseus

FACT: Flies over the surface of the water in search of prey on the surface or just below. Never lands on water.

Status
Common

LENGTH   43 centimetres (17 inches)

HABITAT | THREATS

Northern Fulmar

BEHAVIOUR
- Alternates flapping with gliding
- Stiff, paddle-like wings, looks like flying torpedo
- Rests on water like floating basket, very wide.
- Feeds on surface of water with occasional dives
- Loud low-pitched quack when competing for food, chuckling and grunting

1 Thick yellow beak with black patch

2 Large, round head and thick neck

3 Body white overall with grey back

4 Long wing feathers

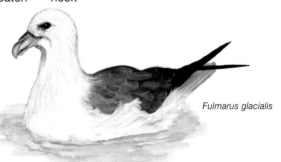

Fulmarus glacialis

Status

Common
- *Numbers falling in recent years*

FACT: Buoyant body shape allows bird to float on surface even during severe storms and high seas.

LENGTH 49 centimetres (19 inches)

HABITAT   **THREATS**

Northern Gannet

BEHAVIOUR
- Dives into water from heights of 20 metres (60 feet)
- Follows schooling fish and feeding whales
- Often flies in line formation
- Alternates flapping and gliding
- Voice is *croaks* and *grunts* heard only on breeding grounds
- Large flocks in spring and summer

1 Body white overall **2** Gold-buff cap on head **3** Black wing tips **4** Long, pointed tail and wings

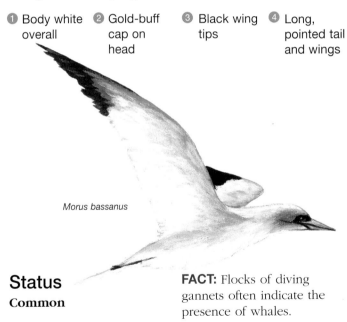

Morus bassanus

Status
Common

FACT: Flocks of diving gannets often indicate the presence of whales.

LENGTH 1.2 metres (3.9 ft)

HABITAT   THREATS

Great Cormorant

BEHAVIOUR
- Body floats low with head tilted slightly above water
- Leaps out of water in order to dive deeper
- Fly-dives and swims underwater
- Flies in straight line with steady wingbeat

① Slightly hooked beak, orange pouch

② Upper ridge of bill level with forehead

③ Large head

④ Large body black overall

Phalacrocorax carbo

FACT: The biggest difference between the two cormorants is head size: Double Crested Cormorant's head is as thick as neck, Great Cormorant's head is thicker.

Status
Protected

LENGTH 1 metre (3 ft)

HABITAT

THREATS

Double-crested Cormorant

BEHAVIOUR
- Body floats low with head tilted above water
- Dives from surface without leaping out of water
- Fly-dives and swims underwater
- Flies in straight line with steady wingbeat

1 Slightly hooked beak, orange pouch

2 Small head on long, snaky neck

3 Slender body black overall

4 White down on belly

Phalacrocorax auritus

FACT: When migrating or flying in large groups, cormorants fly in a "V" formation much like Canada Geese, only less defined.

Status
Protected

LENGTH 89 centimetres (33 inches)

HABITAT

THREATS

Common Eider

BEHAVIOUR
- Opens wings slightly and moves forward when diving
- Swims in large rafts of ducks on open water
- Female quacks. Male moans, during breeding only

1 Long, greenish-grey slopping beak

2 Head shaped like soup ladle with dark crown, long neck

3 Large male has black underparts, white back, breast, head

4 Female body brown overall

Somateria mollissima

Status

Common
- *Recent oil spills and pollution have affected populations*

FACT: Breeds in the Estuary and Gulf of St. Lawrence and winters in Nova Scotia and New England.

LENGTH 68 centimetres (27 inches)

HABITAT   **THREATS**

Herring Gull

BEHAVIOUR
- Lowers head when calling
- Scavenges behind fishing vessels
- Steady wingbeats followed by mostly gliding
- Loud call *kuk-kuk-kuk yucca-yucca-yucca*, among others
- Dives for food on surface of water, submerges head only

1 Body white overall

2 Light grey back, wings with black tips

3 Yellow bill with red spot near tip of lower mandible

4 Feet and legs pink or flesh coloured

Larus argentatus

FACT: Preys on nesting colonies of endangered terns.

Status
Common

LENGTH 66 centimetres (26 inches)

HABITAT

THREATS

Great Black-backed Gull

BEHAVIOUR
- Dominates all other gulls, very aggressive
- Waits near other birds for opportunities to steal food
- Voice is very deep and guttural, *keeeow*

1 Largest gull, with black back and upper-side wings

2 Yellow beak

3 White head, chest and belly

4 Underside of wings white with black/grey wing tips

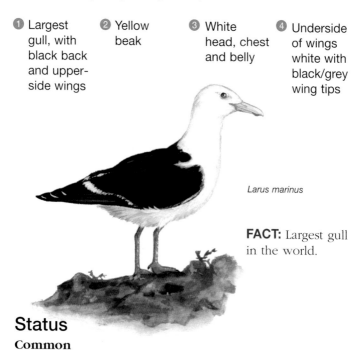

Larus marinus

FACT: Largest gull in the world.

Status
Common

LENGTH 76 centimetres (30 inches)

HABITAT | **THREATS**

Common Tern

BEHAVIOUR
- Quick wingbeats, fast flying
- Fly-dives into water after prey
- Attacks intruders in nesting grounds
- Voice is *kip-kip-kip*, and *teeaar*

1 Black cap **2** Orange-red bill with black tip **3** White overall with long black-tipped wings **4** Forked white tail revealed in flight

Sterna hirundo

Status

Protected

- *Many colonies threatened by predation of introduced animals such as rats*

FACT: Fishermen sometimes follow terns in order to find large schools of fish.

LENGTH 40 centimetres (16 inches)

HABITAT   THREATS

Wilson's Storm-Petrel

BEHAVIOUR
- Hovers at surface with feet dangling in water, wings above head
- Stiff paddle-like wingbeat
- Flies straight with quick wingbeats
- Attracted to lights of fishing vessels
- Voice is soft, peeping when feeding
- Nests in dense, underground colonies on coastal islands

1 Sleek black body with hints of brown

2 Small bird with pointed wings

3 White band running along base of tail

4 Tail is angled in "V" shape in flight

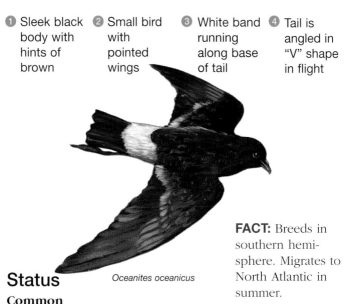

Oceanites oceanicus

FACT: Breeds in southern hemisphere. Migrates to North Atlantic in summer.

Status
Common

LENGTH 18 centimetres (7 inches)

HABITAT | THREATS

Razorbill

BEHAVIOUR
- Short wings can be used for 'flying' underwater
- Floats like a duck with tail cocked upward
- Quick, stiff wing beat

1 Large, stout black bill with white stripe

2 White on chest, belly and under wings

3 Large head has white line from bill to eye

4 Pointed tail, often cocked

Alca torda

FACT: Spends autumn and winter at sea, only coming ashore to breed in colonies, in spring.

Status
Common

LENGTH 43 centimetres (17 inches)

HABITAT

THREATS

Black Guillemot

BEHAVIOUR
- Flutters in flight, back and forth movement
- Very fast flyer
- In winter, plumage changes to light grey and white

1 Black overall, including beak

2 Round white patch on sides of wings

3 Orange legs and feet

4 Short, black tail

Cepphus grylle

Status
Common

FACT: Known as the "sea pigeon" because it is so frequently sighted.

LENGTH 36 centimetres (14 inches)

HABITAT

THREATS

Atlantic Puffin

BEHAVIOUR
- White under wings in flight
- Very fast flyer
- Top heavy, often topples when landing
- Voice is deep, throaty *purrs* and *croaks*

1 Distinctive large, colourful triangular bill

2 Black collar and back against white face

3 Small, round bird with very short tail

4 Bright orange feet and legs

Fratercula arctica

FACT: Can carry many small fish at the same time, making appearance slightly different around the beak. Known as the "Clown of the Sea".

Status

Common
- *Most populations nest on islands in burrows*

LENGTH 30 centimetres (12 inches)

HABITAT | **THREATS**

Arctic Tern

- Wingtips not black as with other terns
- High-pitched voice
- Rarely seen on land except near nests, when they will attack fiercely to defend their colony

Sterna paradisaea

LENGTH **30 cm (12 inches)**

Cory's Shearwater

- Glides close to surface of water and banks back and forth
- Prefers warm water
- Forages for food at night
- Rarely follows ships in search of food

Calonectris diomedea

LENGTH **50 cm (20 inches)**

Manx Shearwater

- Flies with bursts of quick wingbeats followed by long glides
- Visits its nesting islands only at night
- Can travel very long distances

Puffinus puffinus

LENGTH **35 cm (14 inches)**

Long-tailed Duck (Oldsquaw)

- Feathers change colour almost continually from April to October, so has at least four different appearances
- The male's call is pleasantly melodious, like a cross between yodelling and baying

Clangula hyemalis

LENGTH **42 cm (16 inches)**

Black-legged Kittiwake

- Grey wings with black triangles at wing tips
- Only gull that dives and swims underwater to capture food

Rissa tridactyla

LENGTH **40 cm (16 inches)**

Leach's Storm-Petrel

- Flies in zigzag motion with extremely long wings that are pointed and bent
- Tends to be quiet out at sea, but has a high-pitched scream during breeding

Oceanodroma leucorhoa

LENGTH **20 cm (8 inches)**

Index